Letts

KS2

VISUAL REVISION GUIDE

SUCCESS

ICT

Author

Maxine Pountney

CONTENTS

INTRODUCTION TO ICT

GRAPHICS

MULTIMEDIA

Only if you say cheese!

can you take a picture of me and my new mouse

INTERNET & EMAIL

DATABASES AND SPREADSHEETS

MODELLING

CONTROL AND MONITORING

TEST, ANSWERS AND GLOSSARY

WHAT IS ICT?

INFORMATION

ICT stands for Information and Communication Technology.

 **I** stands for information.
All of these pieces of <u>hardware</u> provide information.

To understand more clearly what that means, look at the images here.

video player

television

calculator

radio

CD and DVD

internet

COMMUNICATION

C stands for <u>Communication</u>.

You use all of these pieces of hardware to communicate with others.

e-mail

telephone

fax (facsimile)

mobile phone

TECHNOLOGY

T stands for Technology.

These are all examples of technology hardware.

computer

digital camera

scanner

laptop computer

Hi! I'm Sam. We've got a new interactive Whiteboard in school.

Hello! I'm Mel. Now you'll have to learn to interact instead of just acting up!

QUICK TEST

1. What does **ICT** stand for?

2. Which type of hardware is a **mobile phone**?

3. What is a **laptop**?

ANSWER 1. Information and Communications Technology. **2.** Communication. **3.** A computer.

HAVE A GO ...

Look around your home and your school. Can you see any other pieces of equipment that could fit into these boxes?

CAN YOU COMPUTE?

HARDWARE AND SOFTWARE

Computers are used in many homes and all schools.

The programs you use to help you write, draw or find information, including CD-ROMs, are called software.

CD-ROM/DVDs

floppy disk

All the equipment that is linked to the use of ICT is called hardware.

Here are some names you should know.

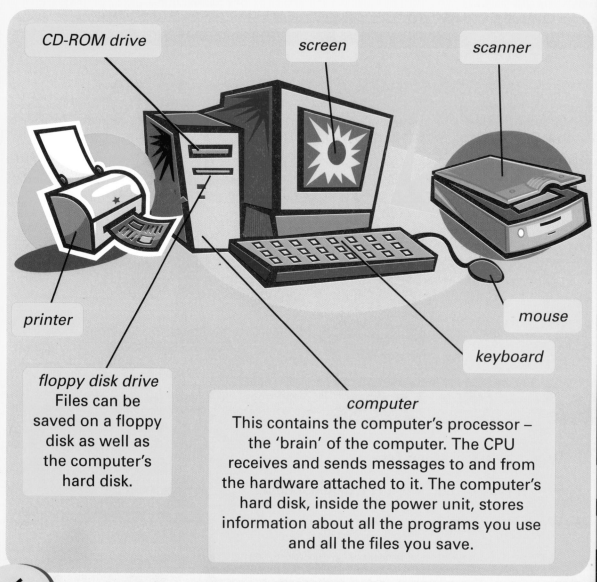

CD-ROM drive

screen

scanner

printer

mouse

keyboard

floppy disk drive
Files can be saved on a floppy disk as well as the computer's hard disk.

computer
This contains the computer's processor – the 'brain' of the computer. The CPU receives and sends messages to and from the hardware attached to it. The computer's hard disk, inside the power unit, stores information about all the programs you use and all the files you save.

THE KEYBOARD: A QUICK TOUR

When you are working at the computer you will use some keys more often than others.

The <u>word processing</u> section will remind you how to use them.

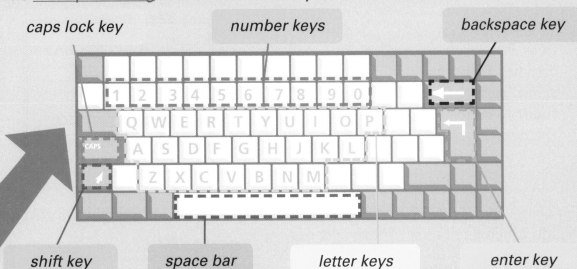

caps lock key number keys backspace key

shift key space bar letter keys enter key

Can you find your way around the computer?

Easy! Turn left at the desk and go straight on.

QUICK TEST

1. Where can you save files?

2. What is a CPU?

3. How do you type a ? ?

ANSWERS 1. On the computer's hard disk or a floppy disk. 2. This is a processor. It is the brain of the computer. 3. Hold the Shift key and press the ? key.

HAVE A GO ...

Look at your computer. Can you name all the 'bits and pieces'? If there's any you're not sure about, ask someone who knows, like a parent, older brother or sister, or a teacher! Check that you can find your way around the keyboard .

TEXT VERSUS HANDWRITTEN

In school and at home you probably do lots of writing. Sometimes you write with a pen or a pencil and sometimes you use a computer. You write for lots of different reasons and for lots of different people. Here are some examples.

> Dear Mr. Smith,
> Sam has to leave school early today to go to the dentist.

> Dear Gran,
> Thank you so much for the lovely birthday present. It was just what I wanted.
> Love Mel

> **SCHOOL SPORTS DAY**
>
> **Egg and spoon
> 2pm**
>
> **Three-legged race
> 2:30pm**

For each example you could use a pen or a computer, but it isn't always easy to decide which one to use. These lists may help.

Handwriting

1. It's more personal.
2. It can be quick to do.
3. But it's not easy to change mistakes ...
4. You can see all your corrections.
5. You can't add anything you've missed out.

Computer

It's easy to read.

You can check spellings.

Corrections can't be seen.

You can easily change mistakes.

You can add things later.

BACK TO BASICS

I'm word processing instead of handwriting.

I wish you were thought processing instead of speaking!

8

WHAT ARE WP AND DTP?

The computer program you use for writing is called a word processor, so when you are writing with a computer you are word-processing. The sentences and words on the screen are called text. Most computers let you choose the font, size and colour for your text.

To make your text look more interesting, you can add Clip Art and photos and move bits around to change the way it looks. This is called desk top publishing or DTP. DTP lets you move and change the text, pictures and the layout on a page to present your writing in different ways. Newspapers and posters are good examples of DTP.

top tip

Use WP (word-processing) and DTP tools for writing stories, poems and letters, or to help yu design magazines, books, newspapers and even web pages.

QUICK TEST

1. Which computer program is used for writing?

2. What is DTP?

3. What is a good example of DTP that is read every day?

HAVE A GO ...

Design a card for someone's birthday. Think about where you will put the pictures and the words.

GETTING AROUND

FINDING YOUR WAY AROUND

When you open a word-processor you will see a page like this.

Drop down menus and Icons or Buttons. The Buttons are shortcuts for writing, printing, saving and editing.

The name of the document. A document won't have a name until you save it.

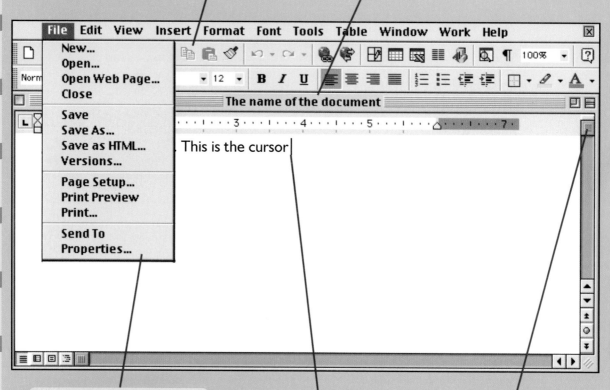

File | Edit | View | Insert | Format | Font | Tools | Table | Window | Work | Help

New...
Open...
Open Web Page...
Close

Save
Save As...
Save as HTML...
Versions...

Page Setup...
Print Preview
Print...

Send To
Properties...

The name of the document

This is the cursor

Each Drop down menu, contains choices or options. Two important options on the **File Menu** are **Save** and **Print**.

The Cursor marks the place where you can add something to the writing on screen. It flashes on and off so you can find it easily.

Use the Scroll Bars to move up and down the page.

If I take three paces back, I wonder if I can delete Sam?

I'm irreplaceable!

top tip

Open a writing program by clicking an icon on the desktop or selecting it from the start menu. Close programs by clicking the cross in the top corner of the screen.

JUST TYPE

When you start a new piece of writing, get your ideas on the screen first. Don't worry about making mistakes – you can <u>edit</u> them later.

Starting a new line

Look at these pieces of writing and see if *line breaks* are needed.

The children went for a walk. It was a nice day so they decided to go to the beach. They loved beachcombing and often came home with lots of treasures.

'You need some clothes for school' says mum.¶

'Your others are too small.'¶

But Sam just wants to stay at home.¶

He hates the shopping mall.¶

For the school trip we need:¶
- a packed lunch¶
- a raincoat¶
- a pair of wellingtons¶
- spare socks.¶

This text is called *running text*. There are no line breaks. You do not need to use the **Enter key** ⌐Enter .

These texts need line breaks.

If a poem, a list or a new paragraph in a story needs a new line, use the **Enter key** ⌐Enter .

QUICK CHANGES

It's easy to make mistakes when you type. Look for the ones in this sentence. Notice they have red or green wavy lines underneath them. Red wavy lines show a spelling mistake and green a grammatical error.

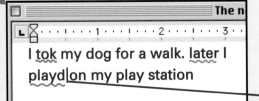

I tok my dog for a walk. later I playd on my play station

Use the **Backspace key** ←Backspace to delete mistakes you notice as you type. Put your **Cursor** to the right of a mistake using the mouse, *delete the error* and *retype* the correct letter.

QUICK TEST

1. How do you get a line break?

2. Which key deletes mistakes?

3. What is running text and when do you use it?

ANSWERS **1.** Press the enter key. **2.** The Backspace key. **3.** Running text means you haven't used the Enter key for line breaks. Use running text when writing a story, but remember, use the Enter key for a new paragraph.

HAVE A GO ...

Type some information about yourself – don't worry about mistakes you can correct them later. The idea is to get used to using your computer.

HIGHLIGHTING

Good writers regularly <u>edit</u> their text to *improve their writing*. They change some words. They move bits of text from one place to another to make it *read better*. They also correct *spelling* and *punctuation*.

You can do this too.

First you need to highlight the text you want to change.

Practise highlighting groups of words. *Hold down the left mouse button and drag the mouse pointer across the text.* When you release the mouse button, the text will stay highlighted. Now just *type in your changes*.

MAKING CHANGES

LOOKING GOOD

Look at this text. *Font*, *colour* and *size* have all been used to give it *extra effect*.

rainbow **big** *go* stairs

Changes are quick and simple using the *shortcut buttons* on the tool bar.

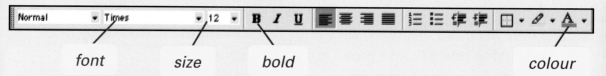

font   size   bold   colour

Highlight the text you want to change first, then change it to make it big, bolder and a different colour or font. Remember to *save your work regularly*, especially when you make any changes. If you want a 'before' and 'after' copy give the changed work a *new filename*.

I've got highlights!

Does that mean I can change you for something else?

★top tip
A speedy way to change one word is to double click on the word and it will be highlighted.

CUT AND PASTE

When redrafting work, you often need to move chunks of text. **Cut** ✂ and **Paste** 📋 lets you do this.

Sam was writing instructions for making a jam sandwich, but realized when he had finished that he needed to put his last instruction first.

- Butter the bread.
- Spread the jam on top of the butter.
- Cut into quarters.
- You need bread, jam and butter.

First he highlighted the text he wanted to move. Then using the **Shortcuts** on the **Toolbar**, he cut ✂ the last line, moved the **Cursor** to the top of the list and pasted 📋 it .

NEW WORDS FOR OLD

If you have used a <u>Thesaurus</u> in school, you will know that it helps you to find lots of different ways of saying the same word.

Many word-processors have a Thesaurus and it is used for exactly the same reason. Highlight the word to be changed and find the Thesaurus – it's usually on the **Tools menu**. Replace the original word with an alternative.

Sometimes it's necessary to change the same word all the way through a piece of writing. **Find and Replace**, in the **Edit menu**, is used for this.

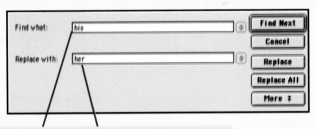

Here the word '**his**' is replaced with '**her**'.

QUICK TEST

1. How can you change the look of your writing?

2. How can you change a group of words?

3. How do you move chunks of text?

ANSWERS 1. Change the font, colour and size or make it bold. **2.** Highlight them and type some new words. **3.** Use Cut and Paste.

HAVE A GO ...

Make some labels to use in school or around the home. Use different fonts and sizes. Think carefully about the colours to use. For example you might use red on any warning notices such as Do Not Enter My Bedroom.

PICTURE THIS

PICTURES MAKE SENSE

Most information books contain *photos*, *illustrations* or *diagrams*. These things help you to *understand* what is written. They also make a book look more interesting.

When you choose a story book, it is usually because you *like the picture* on the *front cover*. Look at Mel and Sam. Would their conversations be as funny if you couldn't see pictures of them? Probably not!

Think about how to make your work more attractive and interesting by adding photos, illustrations or diagrams.

FINDING THE RIGHT PICTURE

Most computers have a *Clip Art* library of pictures on their <u>hard disk</u>. There are also *Clip Art and photo libraries* on <u>CD-ROMs</u>. The <u>Internet</u> has lots of pictures as well, and many of these can be *downloaded free*.

If you take a picture from the Internet or a CD-ROM, *save it and give it a filename* just like any other piece of work. Save it in a folder where it can easily be found again.

Mum wants to take my picture with her new digital camera.

I'd better show her where the delete button is!

★★★★
★top tip★

Use scanned pictures or photos taken with a digital camera for that personal touch in a piece of writing, or add a picture that has been drawn in a paint program.

ADDING A PICTURE

Mel has been making a page for her school magazine. She found two of these pictures in the computer's Clip Art library by searching for animals. To add the pictures to the magazine, she 'clicked' on the picture in the Clip Art library.

She found the third picture on the Internet and saved it as a file in her folder (check out the Internet section to find out how to do this).

This time, to add the picture she chose, **Insert a Picture from File** using the drop down menu.

How to look after your pet

BIG OR SMALL?

Pictures are often the wrong size when added to a page. To adjust the size:

- Click the right mouse button and choose **Format Picture**.
- Choose **Layout** and select an option – **Tight** or **Square** works well for most pictures.
- Drag a corner handle to make the picture bigger or smaller
- Drag a side handle to make it fatter or a handle at the top or bottom to make it long and thin.

It's a lot of fun practising with different effects!

top handle

side handle

corner handle

QUICK TEST

1. Where can you find pictures to add to a piece of writing?

2. Where are the options that let you add pictures?

3. Can you insert pictures that have been saved on a disk?

HAVE A GO ...

Design a page for a class magazine about food – your favourite food! Insert a picture from Clip Art, add a title and write two sentences.

15

GOOD DESIGN

A *graphic designer* **combines** *text and pictures* **to design:** *brochures, posters, tickets, T-shirts, signs and logos.* **But remember, things can't just look cool; they have to work as well. The information needs to be clear and easy to understand, but can look cool too!**

This *menu card* **looks great and you can see where everything is straight away.**

LEFT, RIGHT OR CENTRE?

Look at a *letter, a poster or a brochure.*

Some blocks of text have been moved to the left, some to the right, and some are in the centre or across the page. This is called *alignment.*

Left alignment:
the text has a *straight edge* **and a** *jagged right edge.*

Right alignment:
the text has a *straight edge* **and a** *jagged left edge.*

Centred text:
the text is placed in the *middle of the line* **with an** *equal space on either side.*

To align any text, *highlight it,* **then** *choose* **one of these from the** **tool bar.**

Left alignment   **Right alignment**   **Centred text**

GRAPHIC DESIGN

MAKING IT WORK

Collect all the information you need for your work, including text and pictures.

Type any text into a new document.

Try moving the text around. Change the colour, font, size and alignment to see what looks best.

Add the pictures and shuffle things again by cutting, pasting, moving and resizing.

Experiment until the page looks really good.

Friday 11th
July 2pm

School Field

Splat the Rat,
Treasure Hunt,
Sweet Stall, Bouncy Castle,
Raffle

Come and join the fun

Entry free

Shall I put sea food on the menu?

★ top tip ★

To check the layout, use zoom on the Toolbar, or View Full Screen from the menu bar to see the whole page.

Yes please, see food and eat it.

QUICK TEST

1. What is alignment?

2. The party is at 7 o'clock in the evening on Friday . What's missing?

3. How can you see the layout of the whole page?

ANSWERS **1.** The position of the text on the page. **2.** The date. **3.** Click on 100% Zoom and choose Whole Page.

HAVE A GO ...

Design a menu card for a special party – maybe a bonfire party. List starters, main courses and desserts. Add time, date and place, and some pictures. Think about your readers – is the menu for children, adults or both?

MAKING LISTS

Bullets **and** Numbering **are used for** lists. **They help you to organise your** thoughts.

Compare this…	…to this	…or this
For our school trip we need a packed lunch, a raincoat, a pair of wellingtons and spare socks.	School trip: • packed lunch • raincoat • pair of wellingtons • spare socks.	School trip: 1 packed lunch 2 raincoat 3 pair of wellingtons 4 spare socks.

Bullets **and** Numbers **are** formatting **options in the** menu box, **but there are** shortcuts **on the** Toolbar. **You can use bullets on** posters, **in** report writing **and for** instructions.

FINISHING TOUCHES

CHECKING SPELLINGS

Sam has finished writing a story, but there are lots of typing mistakes.

Correct spelling is very important. Before a book is printed, editors and proof-readers correct spelling mistakes. Sam has to correct his own. For help he uses the computer's Spellchecker in the **Tools menu**. Sam looks through the computer's suggestions, selects the correct spelling, then selects **Change**. Be careful: the first suggestion is not always the right one. Also, the spellchecker only recognises mistakes. It will not see that Sam put hopped instead of hoped!

A spellcheck box looks something like this: Spelling options are shown in the top window.

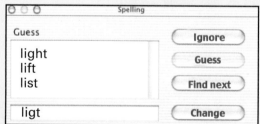

A spellcheck box looks something like this: Spelling options are shown in the top window

Home Alone
The street ligt shone through the wondow of the house. Mel sat there trembling. She hopped someone would come hoime soon. The electrivity had gone off an hour ago and already it was strating to get cold.

NEWSPAPER LAYOUT

Newspapers present text in *boxes* and *columns*. There are DTP tools to do this.

Insert **Text** boxes from the **Insert** menu or **Drawing** toolbar and change the *layout of text into columns* using **Columns** in the **Format** menu, or the **Toolbar** shortcut.

NEWS

Image

Caption

Text box

Columns

DRAWING TOOLS

Some word-processors have simple drawing tools. Look to see if you have some on your word-processor and check out the special effects – *lines, shapes, arrows, diagrams, charts and words!* Have fun.

What's black and white and red all over?

Duh! A newspaper. That's such an old joke!

QUICK TEST

1. When would you use bullets and numbering?

2. What should you do after you have done a spell check on your work?

3. What form does a newspaper take?

HAVE A GO ...

Write a set of instructions for a game using a numbered list – it can be a playground game or a computer game!

WP/DTP INVESTIGATION

NEWSPAPER EDITOR

The Editor has taken the information from his reporters and arranged it on the front page. Compare this page with a real newspaper and an Internet newspaper. Note the editor's use of *headings, columns, pictures*, and the *type of stories* they print. Different newspapers are written for different audiences.

Masthead
The newspaper's *logo*.

Headline
It needs to be *large* and *bold*. The headline for the main story is bigger. The *name of the reporter* is shown under the headline in a smaller size and different font.

Pictures
These pictures were taken by a *digital camera*. Each picture has a *caption* saying what it is.

Stories
Use report writing for *news* or *general interest stories*. Text is *aligned* to fit across each column.

---

the ®Reporter

Hottest Day for 90 years
Written by me

Caption to photograph

Today has been the hottest day since records began 90 years ago. Shoppers sweltered, babies baked and schoolchildren were sent home as temperatures soared into the 30's. Local weatherman, Ivor Mapp, said the good weather is likely to continue until Friday. Not everyone was smiling, though. Tom Digger, a local gardener, was worried about the water shortage. "My potatoes will be ruined if we don't get rain soon!" he sighed.

Local teacher wins lottery

Local teacher, Jane Good, has scooped the lottery jackpot. 'I'll probably have a holiday first' she said. Meanwhile children and teachers from her school tucked into a celebration tea, paid for by Jane of course!

Simple Sun Oil

Advert
Think of the advert as a *small poster*. Notice the aligned text. Use *clip art* and *bullet points*.

DESIGN YOUR OWN NEWS PAGE

A good editor gets all his information together first.

Make a list of what you need for your *front page*.

Look again at real newspapers. How are the front pages designed?

Use your *WP skills* to write two reports. **Think about your audience. Who are you writing this newspaper for? What type of stories will they want to read?**

Use *Clip Art* to make an *advert* to go on your *front page*.

Think of a *name* for your newspaper and *design a logo* using different *fonts* and the *drawing tools*.

PUTTING IT TOGETHER

Put the reports into *two or three columns*. **Think of and add some really** *catchy headlines*. **Insert** *photos* **and** *captions*. **Add an** *advert*. **Cut** ✂ **and Paste** 📋 **to move text and pictures around to make them look good.** *Save your work regularly*, **especially when you make changes. Add a** *logo* **and** *name* **to your newspaper. Finally** *check spellings* **and read everything again.**

I'm trying to write a really eye-catching headline.

How about 'Older sister gives brother sweets?' That would catch my eye!

TEST ROUND-UP

SECTION 1

Finish these sentences.

1. ICT stands for
   _____.

2. All the bits and pieces of equipment are called
   _____.

3. The Shift Key lets you type
   _____.

4. DTP stands for
   _____.

5. A CPU is
   _____.

SECTION 2

Look at these pairs of sentences. What has changed in the second sentence of each pair?

1. Red means stop and green means go.
   Red means STOP and green means GO.
   _____

2. Scary stories look good in scary writing.
   Scary stories look good in scary writing.
   _____

3. Small, smaller, smallest.
   Small, smaller, smallest.
   _____

SECTION 3

Would you use a computer to write any of these?

	Yes	No	Maybe
1. A shopping list reminder.	☐	☐	☐
2. A story.	☐	☐	☐
3. The front page of a newspaper.	☐	☐	☐
4. A note to the teacher.	☐	☐	☐
5. A poster advertising a school club.	☐	☐	☐

SECTION 4

What are these used for?

1. spellchecker _____

2. thesaurus _____

3. cut and paste _____

4. search and replace _____

5. clip art _____

6. alignment _____

7. bullets _____

8. columns _____

9. text boxes _____

10. scanners _____

GET WITH THE PROGRAM

WHAT ARE GRAPHICS?

The computer program you use for *drawing* and *painting* is called a *graphics program*. The images you design or create are called *graphics*.

Drawing tools are lots of fun to use. Using ICT makes it easy to *correct mistakes* and explore new ways to *draw and paint*. With practice, you can copy the style of other artists or create your own pictures.

Good examples of computer–generated graphics include *logos, illustrations, banners and buttons*. Use your own graphics to illustrate your writing, as buttons on <u>multimedia</u> pages, to add colour to your <u>PowerPoint</u> presentations or for <u>DTP</u> artwork.

★ ★ ★ ★
top tip
To draw a perfect horizontal, vertical, or 45-degree diagonal line, hold the Shift key while using the Straight Line tool.

I'm going for the Mondrian look.

I'm more of a Seurat fan – that spray paint effect!

DRAWING AND PAINTING TOOLS

Look at the illustration carefully to see what each tool does. Click a tool to use it, then start creating. To change the *thickness of the line, the shape of the brush* or the *look of the block shapes*, use the **Option Toolbox** underneath the main toolbox.

Rubber
This is for *rubbing out*. Use it with care. If you make a mistake, it's better to use Undo from the Edit menu.

Dropper
This lets you *pick up a colour* and *use it again in another part of the picture*. It's useful when you want an exact colour match.

Pencil
Hold and drag to draw.

Spray Can
Select colour then *click, hold* and *drag* to spray colour.

Straight Line
Drag the *mouse pointer* to *draw a straight line*.

Zoom
This makes your picture *larger*.

Paint Brush
Hold and drag to paint. Change the *shape of the brush* and the *colour* for different effects.

Text
This lets you *add writing* to the picture. You can change the *font, size* and *colour*.

Curved Line
Drag the mouse pointer to *draw a line*. Click and drag points, either one or two, on the line where you want *curves*.

Shapes
Click, hold and drag to draw different shapes; circles, ellipses, rectangles, squares and polygons.

QUICK TEST

1. What are graphics?

2. If the whole page or more than one shape fills with colour when you use the Paint Can, what should you check?

3. What is the easiest way to correct a mistake immediately?

ANSWERS 1. Computer-drawn images. **2.** Check for any gaps in the shape that have 'leaked'. **3.** Use Undo on the edit menu.

HAVE A GO ...

Use the tools to draw some pictures in various styles and create your own gallery. Experiment with warm and cool colours, and compare them.

SPECIAL EFFECTS

REPEAT PATTERNS

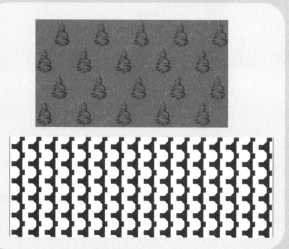

Copy  and **paste** are really useful tools in the **Edit** menu box. Here they have been used to *develop a pattern*. The original drawing was **copied**, then pasted next to the original. The **pasted** image was positioned using **click and drag** to make a pattern. You can create this effect with *stamps* or *Clip Art* as well.

Repeat patterns are used on *carpets, wallpaper, wrapping paper* and in many types of *artwork* such as *Islamic art*.

It's getting dark – can you draw the curtains?

Give me a pencil then!

★ **top tip**

Use 'Save as' and diffe
filenames to keep draf
your drawings in case
need to go back to the

26

SPECIAL EFFECTS

You can create *special effects* by **copying** and **pasting** part of a drawn *picture*, a *digital photo* or a *scanned photo*.

Here's one in the style of *Picasso*.

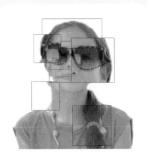

Here's one in the style of *David Hockney*.

Now try *resizing images*. Find the **handle** – a diagonal arrow – at the *bottom right corner* of the pasted image and *drag it* to make the image smaller or larger. Page 15 will help you do this.

The fish in the tank were **copied**, **pasted** and *resized*.

MORE SPECIAL EFFECTS

Once you have created an image, you can make some wonderful <u>symmetrical</u> patterns or pictures by using the options on the **Image** menu.

To make a *symmetrical pattern*, design a repeat pattern, **Copy**, **Paste** then **Flip** it vertically.

To make a collage of pictures in the style of *Andy Warhol*, **Copy** and **Paste** the original image to make a pattern, then use **Colours** or **Invert colours**.

QUICK TEST

1. How do you make a symmetrical pattern?

2. How do you resize an image?

HAVE A GO ...

Design a CD cover for your favourite band or singer using the Special Effects tools.

27

GRAPHIC INVESTIGATION

MAKING PLANS

Drawings and *images* can be used to help you *draw plans*.

The school playground at Wentworth School has been resurfaced. The pupils have lost the playground games that were painted on the playground. Now they have a chance to redesign the playground. But they need your help!

Here is a plan of their playground. It is not drawn to scale.

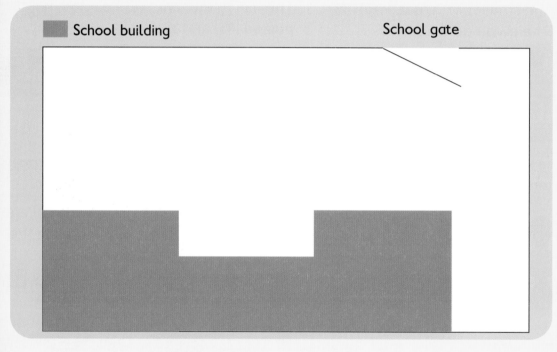

■ School building   School gate

This is the pupils' wish list for their playground.

- Painted playground games.
- Some benches to sit on.
- A quiet area to sit and talk.
- Some tubs with plants.
- A waste bin for crisp packets.

Use a sketch book to help you decide where you are going to put everything. Coloured shapes can represent the different features.

CREATING YOUR DESIGN

Copy the school plan into a Paint program and add the features from your design. What sort of problems do you have? You have probably found that you cannot move and organise the shapes easily.

Now try using a Graphics program. A good Graphics program will let you work in layers. Put the school plan on the background. Now add the features to the second and third layers using the tools on the program to help you to move, rotate and re-size the shapes. By using layers you can move and organise the shapes, and try out different ideas on your background.

AN EXAMPLE PLAN

Here is a completed plan to give you some ideas.

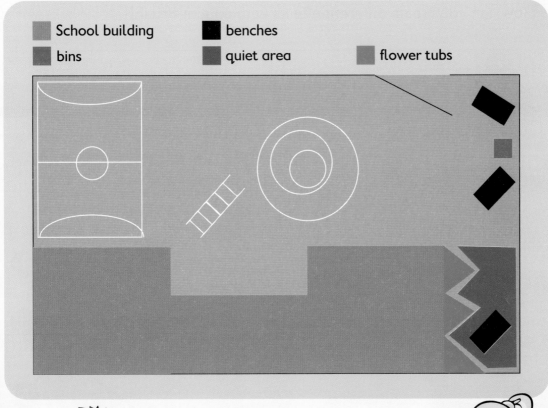

School building   benches
bins   quiet area   flower tubs

I'd wish for a skateboarding area.

And I'd wish for a Sam only area!

TEST ROUND-UP

SECTION 1

1. Give three examples of computer–generated graphics.

   _____

   _____

   _____

2. How do you draw a perfectly straight line?

   _____

3. What does this tool do? 🔲

   _____

4. What does this tool do? ✂

   _____

5. How can you create different effects with a Paint Brush?

   _____

SECTION 2

What are these tools?

1. _____

2. _____

3. _____

4. _____

5. _____

6. _____

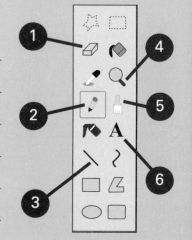

SECTION 3

How do you resize an image on a page?

Put these sentences in the correct order.

1. Now select layout and choose a layout option – tight or square works well for most images – and click OK. ☐

2. Make sure the cursor is over the picture and click the right mouse button. ☐

3. Add an image to a page using a Clip Art Gallery, a digital camera or a scanner. ☐

4. To make the picture bigger or smaller Drag a corner 'handle'. ☐

5. Choose Format Picture from the pop up menu. ☐

SECTION 4

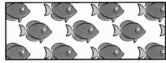 

1. Here is a repeat pattern. How do you create it using a computer?

_____

_____

_____

2. Here is a symmetrical pattern. How do you create it using the computer?

_____

_____

_____

3. Which software program uses layers? Why?

_____

_____

_____

WHAT IS MULTIMEDIA?

When we combine words, pictures and sound in one package, it is called multimedia. CD-ROMs and websites are good examples of multimedia.

You can create your own multimedia pages using presentation and authoring software.

MULTIMEDIA MAYHEM

CD-ROMS

CD-ROMs store huge amounts of information – about 600 million individual pieces of text, sound, still pictures, video and animation. They are popular as dictionaries and encyclopedias because they can hold so much information. They are also used for games, music, Clip Art, story books – in fact, anything that uses multimedia.

CD-ROMs nearly always have a contents page and an index. The index is used in the same way as it is in books – to find key information.

The information on CD-ROMs can be stored in different ways. To help you find the information, most CD-ROMS have pictures on the screen or buttons on the menu bar that link one piece of information with another. CD-ROMs such as dictionaries and encyclopedias also have special search tool buttons.

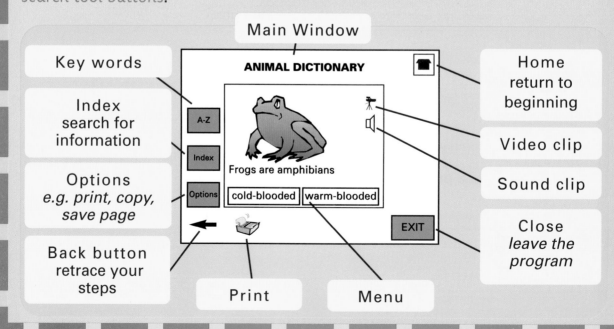

Main Window

Key words

Index search for information

Options e.g. print, copy, save page

Back button retrace your steps

ANIMAL DICTIONARY

A-Z

Index

Options

Frogs are amphibians

cold-blooded | warm-blooded

EXIT

Home return to beginning

Video clip

Sound clip

Close leave the program

Print

Menu

FINDING INFORMATION

To search for information use the following.

- the **Menu** is usually on the home page. It is a *guide* to the CD-ROM.
- the **Index** shows all the *topics* found on the CD-ROM.
- **Key Words** contains a list of *important words*. Some CD-ROMs let you type more than one word for a search. For example, information about frogs in an encyclopedia can be found using *amphibians* and *cold-blooded*.

USING INFORMATION

Decide what you want to find out. Carry out a search and read the information.

Text, pictures, illustrations and diagrams can often be copied from CD-ROMs into a word processor. To copy any information, select the information by *pointing and clicking* if it is a picture or by *highlighting* if it is text. Click the *right mouse button* and choose **Copy**. Open the word processor and click **Paste**.

Some encyclopedias have pages and pages of information, so be careful how much you copy and paste. Make sure the text makes sense and rewrite your notes in your own words. There are so many interesting pages on a CD-ROM that it's easy to get lost when searching. Use the **back button** to retrace your steps or the **home button** to return to the menu.

Better pass it on to mum then!

This computer game is too easy for me.

★ top tip ★

Find information quickly on Dictionary and Encyclopedia CD-ROMs by using a Key Word search, but make sure the word or words are spelt correctly.

QUICK TEST

1. What is multimedia?

2. What does CD stand for?

ANSWERS **1.** Multimedia combines a mixture of text, graphics, sound, still and moving images in one package. **2.** Compact Disk – it can store huge amounts of information.

HAVE A GO ...

Use a CD-ROM encyclopedia to search for information about your favourite animal. Make an information booklet using Copy and Paste and a word processor.

LOOKS GOOD

To make multimedia pages you can use special presentation software. Microsoft PowerPoint is a popular and easy presentation program to use.

Presentation software lets you use text, pictures, video and sound on each page. Each page or screen is called a slide. The slides link together to make a slide show. A slide show can be about any subject.

Mel has created a short presentation about frogs. To make her presentation look attractive she has chosen the same background, font and colour scheme on each page. Diagrams, pictures and text have been used to make the pages interesting and easy to read. Many of the Tools in PowerPoint are the same as those used in the WP, DTP and Graphics sections.

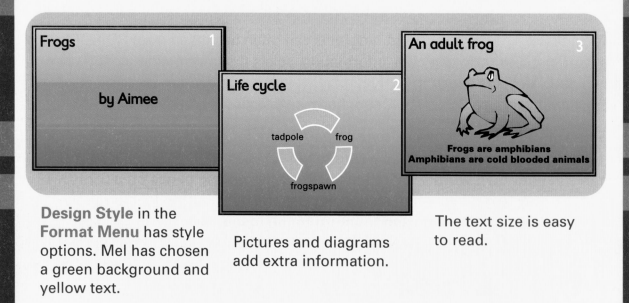

Design Style in the **Format Menu** has style options. Mel has chosen a green background and yellow text.

Pictures and diagrams add extra information.

The text size is easy to read.

To make presentations attractive, use images, photos or pictures from a digital camera, Clip Art or a scanner. For really amazing effects, try short video clips. Use the ones from the computer's Movies or download from the Internet. You could even try making your own with a digital video recorder. Add sound using sound clips or a microphone and the sound recorder built into the computer.

You're spending a lot of time at that computer screen. Have you had your eyes checked.

No, they're still blue!

★top tip★
You can use a template for a new slide, but sometimes it's easier to start with a blank screen and add words, pictures and animation. Remember to use WP, DTP and Drawing tools as well.

PRESENTATION POWER

MAKING THINGS MOVE

One of the most exciting things you can do with presentation software is make things move. This is called *animation*.

Choose the object or the text you want to move by *selecting it with the mouse*. Add an **Effect** using **Custom Animation** on the **Slide Show** menu. There are quite a few to choose from. Try them all to see which looks best.

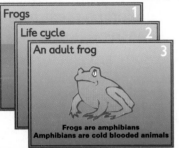

Mel has chosen the order for her images to appear. They are numbered on the screen.

Now she can sit back and run the **Slide Show** by clicking her mouse.

ADDING SOUND

Mel has made her presentations more fun by inserting *sound clips* from the computer's sound clip file. The sounds play when Mel runs the slide show. Adding sound is like adding **Clip Art**. From the **Insert** menu, choose **Movies** 📹 and **Sounds** 🔈.

To record and save your own sounds, use a *microphone attached to a computer* and the **Sound Recorder** in **Accessories**. Make your own sounds using a Music Program – try *www.creatingmusic.com* or *www.bbc.co.uk/radio3/games*.

You can also try downloading sound clips from the Internet. Save sounds as a file. To add them to a slide in *PowerPoint*, choose **Insert Sound** from **File**.

QUICK TEST

1. What is a screen called in PowerPoint?

2. Why is presentation software used for multimedia?

3. How can you add sound to a slide?

ANSWERS 1. A slide. **2.** It lets you use words, pictures, video and animation. **3.** Use sound clips already stored on the computer or record and save sounds using a microphone and Sound Recorder.

HAVE A GO ...

Design a good luck using presentation software, Clip Art, text and sounds.

WEB PAGE WIZARDRY

WEB PAGES AND LINKS

Web pages are used to carry bits of information such as *text, pictures, animation and sound* around the Internet. They are perfect for multimedia. Hyperlinks are used to link the pages together. A link can take you to another page on the website or another site. It can also be a link to a sound or video clip.

Hyperlinks are easy to find if they appear as coloured, underlined text on a page – for example, www.bbc.co.uk or Music Machine. When selected, this type of link changes colour. *Pictures, images and screen buttons* are also used as hyperlinks.

Navigation links and buttons help you find your way around the site. A good example of a navigation link is the **Home button** ⌂. All web pages on a site should have a picture link or a button saying Home. This *takes you back to the first page* of a website – it's very useful if you get lost when browsing!

WEB DESIGN

There are millions of web pages on the Internet, but some look much better than others. Look at this page. See how the colours have been used. The text is very clear. The buttons and links are easy to find and use.

Colourful banner.

Home button.

The menu buttons are hyperlinks to other pages.

Clear, easy-to-read text.

The pictures and words are hyperlinks to other pages.

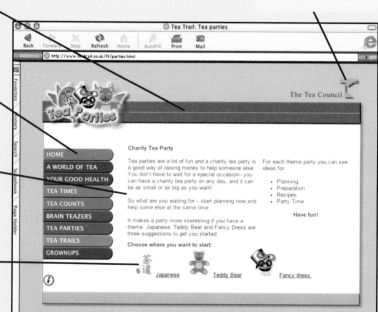

SITES

A collection of web pages is called a website. You can browse pages on a site in any order using the links on the page. Some websites, such as school sites are quite small with only a few pages. Others, such as the BBC website, are very big with lots of pages, sections and links.

Web pages are written in special languages such as html or javascript. This is created using authoring software such as Front Page. You can also create web pages using Microsoft Word by saving your file as a web page.

Why are you so into surfing the net?

Because I don't need to save up my pocket money to buy a board.

top tip

To find a hyperlink, move the Cursor across the screen. When it changes to a hand shape, you've found one.

QUICK TEST

1. What do hyperlinks look like?

2. What should every web page have?

3. What is a collection of web pages called?

ANSWERS 1. Coloured underlined words. Often pictures or buttons are used as hyperlinks. These are harder to find. **2.** A link to the Home Page. **3.** Website.

HAVE A GO ...

Design a Home Page for a school website and decide which buttons to have on the menu as links to other pages.

FAVOURITE STORIES

Think of the best story you have ever heard. The person telling the story may have used sound effects and special voices to make the story more exciting. There might have been pictures in the book that helped you to see what was happening. The story would definitely have had interesting characters and exciting events.

Imagine you are going to tell a story to someone using presentation software. Multimedia can help us you bring your story to life by using sounds, pictures, text and colour.

TELLING STORIES

PLANNING THE STORY

First, you need to choose your story. It should be short and simple, and fit on about six pages. Use one that you know well, such as a traditional fairy tale.

Next, write a plan for the story, saying what happens on each page. This is called a storyboard. It should include a list of pictures and sounds needed.

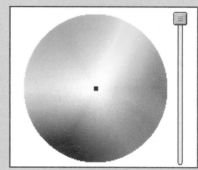

Think about a colour scheme. Use three or four colours that match each other. A colour wheel can help.

Title Page
  Picture: gingerbread
  boy (gb)
  Sound: music
	2 The gb runs away
	  Picture: gb and
	  resized old woman
	  made smaller
		4 The fox carries the
		  gb across the river
		  Pictures: fox and gb
		  Sound: river

1 An old woman makes a
  gb
  Pictures: old woman
  and gb
	3 The gb passes
	  different animals
	  Pictures and sounds:
	  cow, sheep, fox and
	  horse
		5 The fox eats the gb
		  Picture and sound:
		  fox and throaty laugh

38

PUTTING IT TOGETHER

Using *presentation software* to design the screens. Start with a blank screen for each page of the storyboard.

Choose *colours* from the **Format** menu. A light colour works well for the background, with a contrasting colour for the text. Remember, a design style will make each slide look the same.

Insert a text box on each page. Write the *story* inside the text box. Change the *font, size* and *colour* using the **Format Tools**. The sentences and vocabulary should be suitable for your audience.

Add a title to the first page using a different font and size or some word art.

Next add *some pictures* from Clip Art or drawn pictures that have been scanned. Make the pictures move using **Custom Animation**.

Finally, *add some sounds* using the Sound Clips on the computer, or record your own voice.

Do you like the story I've just written?

It's not my type!

top tip

It's more fun to write for an audience. Share your story with children in another class, or a younger member of your family.

QUICK TEST

1. What is a storyboard?

2. What can help you when choosing colours?

3. Where do you put the writing on a presentation screen?

HAVE A GO ...

Create your own short story using presentation software. How does it compare to a story read from a book?

MULTIMEDIA INVESTIGATION

PLANNING

Grange School hasn't got a website. The pupils would like one, but they need your help. There are three classes and they each want some webpages. They also need some school information pages and a Home Page.

This plan shows their ideas so far. The pupils drew their plans on paper first. They used a sheet of paper for each screen page, giving each one a name. They moved their sheets around on a large table to decide how the pages should be linked together.

The lines show you how the pages link together. All the pages need a link to the Home Page. Now you can see why the Internet is called the web!

The pupils have used colour to help with navigation. Green, blue or red have been chosen for class pages. Yellow is for pages used by the whole school.

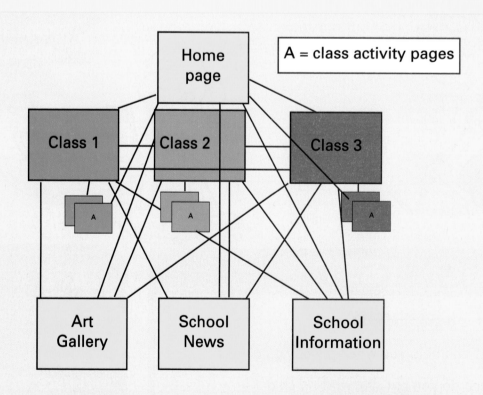

DESIGNING

Help the Grange School pupils to design their pages.

Before you start, use the Internet to look at some school web pages. Which ones look good? Which ones are easy to use? Why? Some may use moving pictures, but you need to think about the basics first.

Grange School needs:
- a banner or logo for each page
- some buttons and words that you can use as hyperlinks to another page
- a colour scheme – pick three co-ordinating colours
- an easy-to-read font and text size
- a simple introduction on the Home Page
- some easy–to–read text on the other pages.

Make some planning pages like the pupils from Grange School and add your ideas. Planning is best done on paper.

PICTURES AND SOUNDS

Find some Clip Art that Grange School could use on its pages. What would they use for the art gallery for example?

Think of any sounds the pupils could use to make their pages more interesting.

There are lots of pages that you could include on a school website, that the pupils of Grange School haven't thought of. You could have a page for writing. What others can you think of? What would you have on your school website?

I'd like to build a website.

I don't see how, when you're scared of spiders!

TEST ROUND-UP

SECTION 1

Tick the correct answer.

1. All web pages on a site should have:
   a. a Home Page link ☐
   b. pictures ☐
   c. sounds ☐

2. Multimedia is:
   a. sound only ☐
   b. a combination of sound, text, animation and video ☐
   c. animation only ☐

3. CD-ROM stands for:
   a. Compact Disk, Remember Our Menus ☐
   b. Compact Disk, Read Only Memory ☐
   c. Computer Disk, Read Only Menus ☐

4. When the mouse pointer passes over a hyperlink on a page, the pointer changes to a:
   a. link ☐
   b. globe ☐
   c. hand ☐

5. When choosing the right colours for page use:
   a. a colour wheel ☐
   b. a cartwheel ☐
   c. a menu box ☐

SECTION 2

Find ten words in this word search that combined mean multimedia.

N	O	T	T	U	B	I	O
A	M	X	S	L	I	D	E
T	E	G	M	I	T	I	G
T	S	O	U	N	D	E	A
A	M	E	S	U	D	M	P
N	I	D	I	A	I	L	B
M	P	I	C	T	U	R	E
E	I	V	O	M	A	N	W

SECTION 3

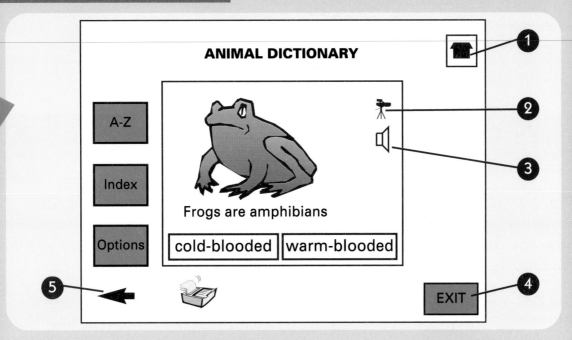

What are the buttons used for on a CD-ROM screen?

1. _____

2. _____

3. _____

4. _____

5. _____

SECTION 4

Are these statements true or false? Write **T** for true and **F** for false.

1. Presentation software lets you use video and sound clips. _____

2. You can record sounds on a computer without a microphone. _____

3. A slide show is made up of web pages linked together. _____

4. Some computers have sound and video clips in a clip organiser. _____

5. Navigation buttons help you to find your way around a website. _____

6. CD-ROMs can hold about 600 million bits of information. _____

WELCOME TO THE WEB

THE INTERNET AND THE WEB

The <u>Internet</u> is made up of *millions of computers* all around the world. The computers are connected by *telephone lines, cables and satellites*. Information from one computer can be shared with all the others using the Internet and the <u>World Wide Web</u>.

The *World Wide Web* (www) is like a *large library* with millions of pages of information. When you connect to the Internet you can visit these pages. Many of them use <u>multimedia</u>.

To link your computer to the Internet you need a *phone line* and a <u>modem</u>. Modems allow computers to talk to each other. Most computers have modems inside them. You also need Internet software such as *Internet Explorer* or *Netscape*.

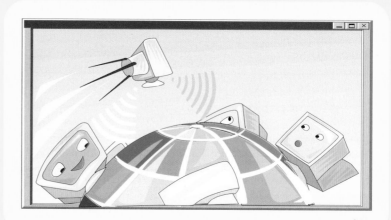

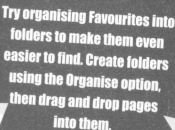

top tip

Try organising Favourites into folders to make them even easier to find. Create folders using the Organise option, then drag and drop pages into them.

Do you know that the Internet never sleeps?

It's available 24/7.

ADDRESSES AND URLS

Every web page has its own address, called an URL (Universal Resource Locator). It is shown in the address box when you visit a website.

The address is like a code to help you get to the right page. Sometimes the address is quite long with symbols such as [/] or [-], but it must be typed accurately or, just like a letter with the wrong address, you won't get there.

Most web addresses start with **http://**, but you only need to type **www.** followed by the address to get to the page you want as the **http://** comes up automatically when you go to a website.

> 🌐 www.lettsed.co.uk

FAVOURITES

There are some web pages that you visit again and again. Perhaps it's a games site, a football team or a school website. These sites are your Favourites.

Instead of typing the address each time, you can create a short cut that lets you get to the site quickly. First look at the **Menu bar** and find **Favourites** or **Bookmarks** – they are the same thing. Visit the page you want to save, choose **Add to Favourites** and it will be added to the list.

Favorites	Tools	Window	Help
Add Page to Favorites			⌘D

So when you want to go to a web page you have saved, open Favourites and choose your page.

> ⬦ Favorites   ▶

QUICK TEST

1. What is the Internet?

2. What do you need to use the Internet?

3. What does it mean if you go online?

ANSWERS 1. Millions of computers all over the world connected together to share information. **2.** A computer, phone line, a modem and some Internet software. **3.** You are using the Internet to receive and send information.

HAVE A GO ...

Connecting to the Internet is called 'going online'. Find four interesting web pages and add them to your Favourites.

45

SEARCH ENGINES

There are millions of web pages on the World Wide Web, so how can you ever find anything? *Search Engines* are special websites that can help you.

Here is an example. Type a word or a few words like 'London' in the **Search box** and press **Search**.

The Search Engine will find lots of websites about London and *give links* to their pages. To find a particular piece of information make the Search more accurate using AND or +. It is important to use just the key words to find the right information. Put the most important *key word first* and remember to *spell the words correctly*.

Search the Web: | London | **Search** | • Advanced
• Preferences

GET INFORMED

HYPERLINKS

A hyperlink or *link* takes you to another page on the website or another website. It can also link you to a *sound or video clip*.

Hyperlinks are easy to find if they appear as coloured, underlined text on a page for example, www.bbc.co.uk or Music Machine. When selected, these links change colour.

Pictures and buttons are often used as hyperlinks. To find these, move the **Cursor** across the screen. When it changes to a *hand shape*, it has found a hyperlink.

You can find out more information about hyperlinks in the Multimedia section (pages 32 – 43).

Sometimes links don't work, because the page has been deleted from the website, or it is being rewritten. If this happens, the message *Page Expired* appears. Click the **Back** [Back] button to return to where you were.

TREASURE TRAIL

Following links is like following a treasure trail. They are clues to where you can go to find out more information. Follow them if they look interesting. But be careful, you could jump to another website. To go back at any time, use the **Back** button.

Let's try a trail now. Go to:

- Yahooligans, www.yahooligans.com
- Search for London. You should have about 60 sites listed.
- Improve your Search by typing London + famous buildings
- Use the sites listed to answer this question: Where is the Royal Opera House?

If your answer is Covent Garden, Well done!
You have become an Internet Detective.

★ **top tip** ★

Here are three useful Search Engines to try:
www.google.co.uk
www.ajkids.com
www.yahooligans.com

I've been making up some web jokes for our school magazine.

I bet they're e-larious!

HAVE A GO ...

Use a Search Engine to find information about your favourite animal. Use AND or + to make the search more accurate. Make up three treasure trail questions about your animal and give them to a friend to answer. Is your friend an Internet detective?

QUICK TEST

1. What are Search Engines?

2. How can you make a search more accurate?

3. Do you have to type a sentence in a Search box?

ANSWERS 1. Millions of computers all over the world connected together to Special web sites that help you find information. **2.** Type AND or + between the key words. **3.** No, just the key words. Put the most important word first.

47

TOOLS

Web pages contain information – text, pictures, sound and video. A browser lets you look at and use the information.

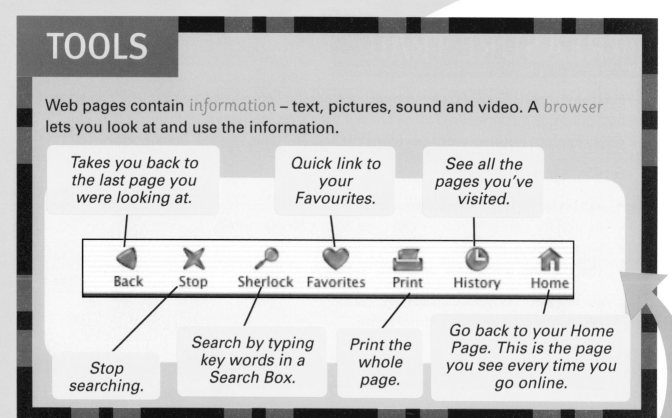

Takes you back to the last page you were looking at.

Quick link to your Favourites.

See all the pages you've visited.

Back   Stop   Sherlock   Favorites   Print   History   Home

Stop searching.

Search by typing key words in a Search Box.

Print the whole page.

Go back to your Home Page. This is the page you see every time you go online.

INSIDE INFORMATION

COPY AND PASTE

To copy any information from an Internet page into a word processor (WP), select the information by pointing and clicking if it is a picture, or by highlighting if it is text. Click the right mouse button and choose **Copy** . Open the word processor and click **Paste** .

It sounds very easy, but sometimes there are problems. The pictures and the writing on the web page have been created using a special code that isn't always easy to copy. Sometimes the pictures on the web are made from a 'collage' of smaller pictures. If copy is used on a collage of pictures, it only copies bits that usually don't look very good in a word processor. Animated pictures can't be copied into a WP. They only work in a web browser.

Copy and Paste

PROJECTS

Web pages can be really useful when researching information for topic work, because there are so many pages and there is so much information. But there are some important rules to remember.

- Check that the information is *up to date and accurate*. Some pages were written a few years ago and they are still there, but the information on them may no longer be correct.
- Check *who has written the web page*. If it is a well known society, group or organisation, their facts are usually right.
- Use *magazines and books* as well as the web to find information. Magazines sometimes suggest web links to try.
- Understand that *some information might be biased*. Some personal web pages, created by one person, reflect their feelings, thoughts and ideas. Read them, but try to use them to develop your own ideas.
- Use the *edit tools in a WP to rewrite any information* you have copied in your own words. Use (DTP) tools to move text and pictures on a page when preparing project work.

I want to look for some new clothes on the web's shopping pages.

How will you try them on?

top tip

If it takes a long time for a web page to open, check that you have typed the address properly.

QUICK TEST

1. Which tool lets you see all the pages you've visited?

2. How do you copy a piece of text from a web page?

3. Is the information on a web page always accurate and up to date?

ANSWERS 1. The History button. **2.** Highlight it, right click the mouse and select Copy. **3.** No.

HAVE A GO ...

Carry out a Search to find out about your favourite author. Copy and paste some information about the author and a photo if possible into a WP. Use this to write the 'blurb' for a book cover.

49

MAKING CONTACT

EMAIL

Email is a way of *quickly sending messages* from one person to another using the Internet.

It's possible to write messages without being *connected* to the Internet, but you have to be connected to *send a message*. You also need to be connected to *receive a message*.

Someone can send you a message anytime, but it will wait in your Mailbox until you next connect to the Internet and open it.

MAILBOXES, ADDRESSES, AND MESSAGES

A Mailbox lets you *send and receive messages*. Everyone who has an email address has a Mailbox.

The Address Book keeps a note of the email addresses you use regularly. Email addresses look like this:

humptydumpty@thewall.com

The first part is the name of the person or a code name. The second part says where their mailbox is. This is all the mailbox needs to know to send a message. The first part and the second part are always seperated by the @ symbol.

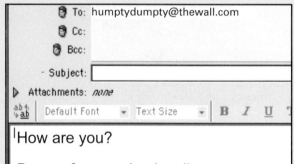

To: humptydumpty@thewall.com
Cc:
Bcc:
- Subject:
Attachments: *none*
Default Font ▼ Text Size ▼ **B** *I* U

How are you?

Do you fancy going bowling on Friday after school? Mum can take us at 5. Let me know.

ATTACHMENTS

Most messages are words, but you can send *pictures, documents, video clips or sound clips* – in fact, anything that has been *saved as a file*. This is called sending an *Attachment*. There is an Attachment option in the Mailbox that lets you do this.

Clicking on the **Add Attachment**  button brings up a **Menu**.

Find the file you want to send and *double click* it to attach it.

You can open attachments that are sent to you if you have the *right software* on your computer, but you can't play music or video clips if your computer doesn't have the right software.

★ top tip ★

If you receive an email with an attachment, make sure it is from someone you know. Many computer viruses attach themselves to email attachments. A virus can damage your files. If in doubt – don't open it!

Do you have to put a stamp on an email?

No, it would make a mess of the screen!

QUICK TEST

1. Where do messages go when you send them?

2. Do you have to be connected to the Internet to send a message?

3. Which symbol do you always see in an email address?

ANSWERS 1. Through the telephone wires to someone's mailbox. **2.** Yes, but you can write a message before you connect and send. **3.** @.

HAVE A GO ...

Send an email to a friend or a relative. Keep the message short, but ask them to reply, so you can practise opening and reading an email.

TAKING CARE

There are lots of exciting things to do on the Internet, but there are some dangers too!

Whenever you use the Internet, you should ask a parent, guardian or teacher to look at the sites you visit. It is possible to put some special software on a computer to stop you going to sites that are just for adults. Many schools use this.

It is also a good idea to take regular breaks from the computer, at least 10 minutes every hour. It is tiring for your eyes and your brain needs a rest.

PLAY IT SAFE

CHAT ROOMS

Chat Rooms are very popular and easy to enter. Many TV shows have Chat Rooms, where you can make comments or ask questions about the programmes.

In a Chat Room, the keyboard is used to chat. Everyone types messages to reply to those already on the screen. It's possible to join a chat just to read what others are saying and not chat yourself.

You should always ask a parent, guardian or teacher if you can use a Chat Room. Remember, you are talking to strangers. So be careful – no matter how nice they seem!

Here are some good rules to follow when 'chatting'.

- Use a nickname.
- Never give personal details such as your name, address, school or phone number.
- Never give any details about yourself or your family.
- Never arrange to meet someone from a Chat Room.
- Never type anything rude or nasty. If you see any nasty comments, tell an adult.

DOWNLOADING

To be able to *see videos or hear sounds* on the Internet you need some special software on your computer called *plug-ins*. Popular plug-ins include *RealPlayer, QuickTime and Flash*.

You can download plug-ins from the web. Plug-in sites give you instructions on how to do this. But you should only download reliable plug-ins and you should always ask an adult first.

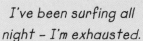

I've been surfing all night – I'm exhausted.

You must be pretty wet as well!

★**top tip**★

Shopping on the Internet is becoming more popular. But you should never order anything from the Internet without an adult's permission.

QUICK TEST

1. What should you do **regularly** when using the computer?

2. What details should you not give out in **Chat Rooms**?

3. What should you use if you enter a **Chat Room**?

ANSWERS 1. Take a break. **2.** Personal details such as home, address, school or phone number. **3.** A nickname.

HAVE A GO ...

Make your own list of safety rules for using the Internet and pin them next to the computer. Include 'Take regular breaks!'

INTERNET & EMAIL INVESTIGATION

CLASS PROJECT

Class 6 has been writing to the pupils in a school in the Netherlands for about three months. Each pupil has an e-pal.

The schools have decided to put together some information about their local area to share with their partner school.

Let's imagine you are in Class 6 and that you are part of this project. Look at this list and put a tick by the thing you think you can do, using a Search Engine.

- Find information about the geography of your local area. ☐

- Find information about the history of your local area. ☐

- Find information about things to do for young people in your local area. ☐

- Find information about interesting places to visit in your local area. ☐

- Find some photos of your local area. ☐

USING EMAIL

Your partner in the Netherlands has written this message to you.

> Subject: Research
>
> ▷ Attachments: *none*
>
> ab | Default Font ▾ | Text Size ▾ | **B** *I* <u>U</u> T | ≡ ≡ ≡ | ⅓≡ ≣ ⅻ ⅻ | A ▾ ◇
>
> |
>
> 'Hi,
>
> Have been doing some research about my town. Found some really interesting stuff! What have you found? I think I'm going to put together a page about some places to visit. What about you? Let me know how you are getting on.
>
> Milo

Reply to Milo's message telling him what you've been up to and what you are thinking of doing for the project.

USING EMAIL

You have decided to make a treasure trail about your local area giving clues, so that the children in the Netherlands can find the answers by searching on the Internet. Look again at the treasure trail on p47.

Design a treasure trail for Milo so he can find out some information about your town. The clues could lead to the name of a famous building, a football team, a place to shop such as a large shopping centre, or a place to visit such as as a museum.

I'd like to learn Dutch.

You don't need to - you speak double dutch already!

TEST ROUND-UP

SECTION 1

Write in the missing link words. Clue: It is the same word that is missing in each pair of sentences.

1. The Internet is made up of millions of _____ . _____ are connected by telephone lines, cables and satellites.

2. Many www pages use _____ . _____ is a combination of text, sound, video and animation.

3. Save a favourite web page by adding it to your list of _____ . _____ are like Bookmarks; they mark a page you want to visit again and again.

4. There are millions of pages on the _____ . The _____ has Search Engine pages to help you find information quickly.

5. Email is sent to a _____ . A _____ lets you send and receive messages.

SECTION 2

What are these?

1. Plug-ins _____

2. Chat Rooms _____

3. Modems _____

4. URLs _____

5. Computer viruses _____

SECTION 3

Spider's web: I have eight letters, what am I? Look at the clues, which each refers to a letter, then work out the word.

My eighth is in button but not in music.

My first is in music, but not in sound.

My second is in sound, but not in Clip Art.

My seventh is in search, but not in button.

My third is in Clip Art, but not in web page.

What is the word?

My sixth is in net, but not in search.

My fifth is in history, but not in net.

My fourth is in web page, but not in history.

SECTION 4

Use www.yahooligans.com and follow links to find answers to the questions.

1. Search Singapore + Art Museum. What is the address of Singapore History Museum?

   _____

2. Search eclipse + lunar. What is a lunar eclipse?

   _____

3. Search Victoria + queen. When was Queen Victoria born and when did she die? How long was she queen?

   _____

4. Search Peru + lost city. What are Nasca lines?

   _____

   _____

A MATTER OF FACT

DATABASES

Data is another word for *facts*. For example, your personal data consists of your name, your date of birth, your address, your eye colour and so on.

A *database* provides a way *to store data*. Questions about the data can be answered quickly and easily by *carrying out a search*, even when there is a huge amount of data.

Telephone directories are databases of names, addresses and telephone numbers. There are thousands of names in one book, but it is easy to find one person, because the names are arranged in alphabetical order. All databases, including computer databases, use a *system to store information that makes them easy to search.*

FIELDS AND RECORDS

Collecting and storing information in an organised way makes it easier to find answers to questions. Information in a *database* is structured into *fields and Records.*

The pupils in Class 1 have been looking at homes and houses for their project. They have collected information and made some record cards. Here is Rosie's record card.

The Field names are shown in blue and Rosie's answers are shown in black. All the pupils completed a record card using the computer and database software. Now they are ready to start asking questions.

Notice on Rosie's record that there are *different field types*. Only one question needs a numerical answer. The others need word answers, but two of these are yes/no answers.

This is important when you are thinking about *Field names*.

Homes and Houses:	
Name:	Rosie
Type of house:	semi detached
Material:	brick
Roof:	tile
Rooms:	6
Garden	yes
Garage	no

top tip

Make a search more interesting by ask a 'double question' For example, how many semi-detached houses in Class 1's database were made of stone?

SEARCH AND SORT

You can ask a database questions using **Search** and **Sort**, but a database can only answer questions if the data has been entered. Class 1's Homes and House database won't tell you which rooms Rosie has in her house – only that she has six rooms.

Here is an example of a database that is used in a primary school. Most databases have options to search and sort.

| Add new record | Delete record | Sheet - + | List | Search | Sort | Save/print |

Select this to see 1 record at a time on the screen. Move through the records using - or +.

Select this to see all records.

Search the database, eg. type stone into the Materials field and click Find All to list all the houses made with stone.

Sort all records or results from a search in alphabetical order.

A collection of records is called a File. On Class 1's computer, they have a file called Homes and Houses. It has everyone's record in it.

You can make records on individual sheets of paper or use a database software program. Which do you think will be quicker when you Search for information?

Facts, facts, facts – there's so much to learn.

Put them in a database, then you only have one thing to worry about!

HAVE A GO ...

Collect information about five garden birds. Make and complete five record cards with these field names: name of bird; colour; size; habitat, migrates.
Sort the birds by colour, then by habitat. How many birds had brown colourings? How many built their nests in hedges? Which birds, if any, migrate?

QUICK TEST

1. What is personal data?

2. How are databases organised?

3. How do you put information into alphabetical order in a database?

ANSWERS 1. Information about yourself. **2.** Into Fields and Records. **3.** Select Sort.

BRANCHING OUT

YES/NO

A branching database helps you to sort and classify information by using simple questions that can be answered with Yes or No. The difficult part is trying to think of the questions!

Look at this tree diagram and follow the branches.

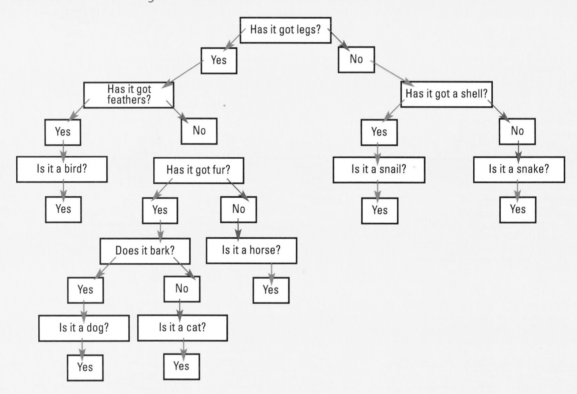

Sam starts with six creatures – a horse, a snail, a snake, a dog, a cat and a bird. He puts their names into a branching database program on the computer, then starts to ask some questions that can only be answered by Yes or No. By asking the right questions, the database helps him to sort them out.

ASKING QUESTIONS

Some questions in the branching database work better than others. Now that Sam has created a file, he can add more creatures. By using the program and the same questions, he can carry on sorting the creatures into groups.

Think of any other creatures that would follow the same branch as the snake. A worm would. Now think of a question to type in to separate the worm and the snake like... Has it got scales?

TREE DIAGRAMS

Tree diagrams and branching databases are effective ways to organise information. Diagrams such as the ones showing Sam's creatures can be created for all sorts of things, such as fruit, trees, animals, food, materials.

The advantage of using a computer branching database is that you can keep adding to it, so you can sort and classify as many types of fruit as you can name, or all the animals you can think of. It would be hard to do that on a piece of paper.

You can also search a branching database by asking multiple questions for example, which creature has fur and legs, but does not bark. On Sam's database it is a cat, but if he adds more creatures, then the database will suggest more answers.

Can't you say anything, but Yes or No when I ask you a question?

No!

★ top tip ★

When making a branching database, think of general questions that will split your things into two groups at the start. Make the questions more exact later on.

HAVE A GO ...

Construct a paper-based branching database on strips of paper to practise asking the right types of questions. Only ask questions that can be answered with yes or no. Use red arrows for no answers and green arrows for yes answers. Start with a set of 10 fruits.

QUICK TEST

1. What are branching databases useful for?

2. Why is a branching database like a tree?

ANSWERS 1. Sorting and grouping information such as things with the same characteristics. 2. It has lots of branches that go in different directions depending on whether the answer is Yes or No.

SPREADSHEETS

A spreadsheet is a grid that organises data into columns and rows. You can type words or numbers into a spreadsheet.

Spreadsheets can be used for calculations, to work out costs and to keep records. They are also pretty good at drawing graphs and charts!

SPREADSHEETS

All spreadsheets have a similar layout and use similar tools.

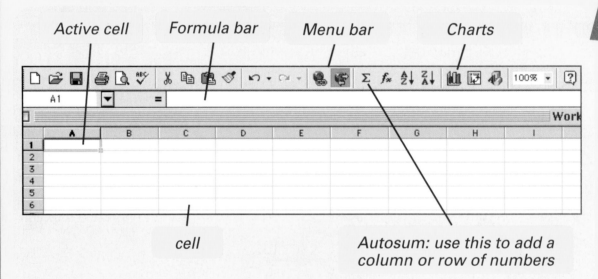

Active cell

Formula bar

Menu bar

Charts

cell

Autosum: use this to add a column or row of numbers

On a spreadsheet, numbers or words are entered into individual cells. The information you type also appears in the **Formula** bar.

Change text size, font and colour using the **Format** tools and put grid lines on the worksheet by adding **Borders**, using the **Format** menu. This table was created using all these tools.

G10	=			
	A	B	C	D	E
1	**Athletic Result**				
2					
3			long jump	high jump	100 meters
4	Collins	Maxine	3.5mm	1.3m	22 sec.
5	Crabtree	Sheila	3.2mm	1.5m	21 sec.
6	Green	Susan	4.1m	1.4m	23 sec.
7	Kelly	Mary	3.4m	1.1m	22 sec.
8	Lacey	Sarah	3.8m	1.8m	21 sec.
9					

SPREADSHEET SUCCESS

CELL REFERENCES

Cell referencing means *giving the name of the cell*. Use these cell references to read the story.

A3, C2, A4, B1, C4, E5, F5, C1, E3, E1, A4 D3, E2, D5, A2, B2, C5, D2.
E4, B4, A1, F2, F5, D5, F3, A6, B6, D6, A5, F4.

	A	B	C	D	E	F
1	she	time	old	was	in	that
2	cottage	on	upon	hill	down	found
3	Once	were	she	broken	woman,	book
4	a	day	there	an	One	fortune.
5	her	a	a	old	lived	an
6	that	would		change		

My teacher said my spreadsheet was the best in the class.

Does that put your work on the best cell-ers list?

QUICK TEST

1. What is a spreadsheet?

2. What does the spreadsheet grid use to organise data?

3. Which cell is to the left of C3?

ANSWERS **1.** A grid that organises data into columns and rows. **2.** Rows, columns and cells. **3.** B3.

HAVE A GO ...

To practice using cell references, write your own spreadsheet story and give the code and cell references to a friend to work out.

CALCULATIONS

Spreadsheets are really useful for helping with simple calculations.

Let's try one. Open a spreadsheet program.

- Type 120 in cell **A1** and 130 in **B1**.
- Click on **C1** to make it the active cell and in the formula bar type = A1+B1 then **Enter** to add them together.

The answer should appear in **C1**. Does it say 250? Well done.

Try this again with different numbers and use:
| − | to subtract | + | to add | * | to multiply | / | to divide.

NUMBER CRUNCHING

FINDING THE SUM

This time try adding numbers in six cells.

- In cells **A1** to **A6** of **column A**, type these numbers: **45, 89, 55, 90, 127, 355**.
- Now add them using the + sign between each cell reference.
- Click on **A7** to make it the active cell and type **=A1+A2+A3+A4+A5+A6**.

What did you get? 761 – excellent! But it took quite some time to type all those cell references, didn't it? A shorter way would be to type **=SUM(A1:A6)**. Try it and see.

Whenever you use = you are using a formula. Spreadsheets use formulae to calculate. Have another go with some more numbers. This time type the numbers across a row. Type in three numbers and in **D1** type **=A1+B1+C1**.

This spreadsheet is helping me with my maths.

I can hear those numbers crunching – ouch!

FUN WITH NUMBERS

Mel has gone shopping. Work out the formula she used to help her calculate how much she paid for the bananas.

Mel uses **Copy** to put this formula to the other cells in **Column D**. Finally she uses **SUM** to calculate the total in **D16**.

She took £10 with her. How much change did she get?

The formula she used for the bananas was **=B5*C5**.

She copied this to all the other cells in **Column D**. Then using **SUM** she found she spent £8.64 leaving her with £1.36.

	A	B	C	D
1				
2	**Shopping List**			
3				
4	item	price each (p)	number bought	cost
5	banana	18	5	90
6	apple	27	4	
7	orange	30	2	
8	milk	27	2	
9	tin of beans	24	3	
10	bread bun	8	6	
11	can of cola	33	4	
12	egg	8	10	
13	yogart	34	4	
14	ice pop	7	12	
15				
16			Total	
17				

★ top tip ★

Autosum is a shortcut tool that's used to add a column or row of numbers. But make sure it is the column or row you want to add – check the cell references in the pop-up menu.

QUICK TEST

1. Which shortcut tool helps you to add a row of numbers?

2. Which symbol means multiply?

3. Which symbol means divide?

ANSWERS **1.** Autosum. **2.** *. **3.** /.

HAVE A GO ...

For more number crunching, type 264 in A2, 15 in B2 and =A2/B2 in C2. Remember to press Enter to get the answer. Type 305 in A3, 44 in B3 and =A3*B3 in C3.

Now try some of your own.

GRAPHS AND CHARTS

GRAPHS ARE HELPFUL

Databases and spreadsheets use data, but sometimes this data can be difficult to understand when it is in lists and groups or grids.

Graphs *simplify the information*. They make it easier to see the whole picture and to answer questions.

Most spreadsheets and databases use *Chart Wizards* 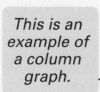.

These guide you through all the steps towards making a graph, but different graphs are used for different purposes.

DIFFERENT GRAPHS

It is important to choose an appropriate graph to suit the purpose of the investigation.

- **Columns or bar graphs**: A column graph is suitable when there are *two or more sets of data*. You could also use a line graph for this, but the columns help you to make comparisons more easily.

- **Pie charts**: A pie chart shows *how things are shared out*, for example, how much money you spend on things.

- **Line Chart**: A line chart shows a change in something *over a period of time*.

This is an example of a column graph.

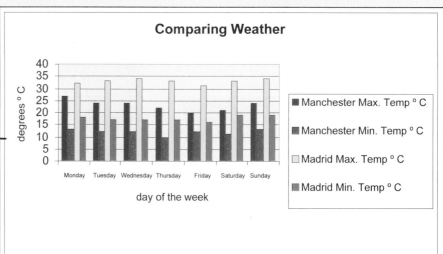

HOW COMPUTERS HELP

A computer makes drawing graphs quick, easy and accurate. The examples here are accurate, because the data was entered very carefully into the spreadsheet and database programs.

If you make a mistake when adding the data, it can alter the shape of your graph. With some graphs you can tell straight away that you have made a mistake, but not always. You will notice if there is a mistake when you start asking questions and using the information on the graph. A computer makes it easy to correct any mistakes. Go back to the spreadsheet, change the figurse and redraw the graph.

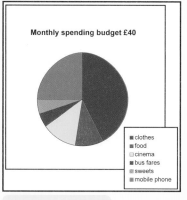

a pie chart

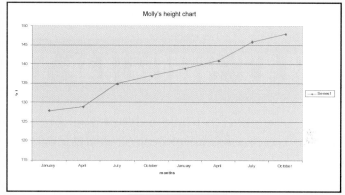

a line graph

I'm going to keep my spending money on a spreadsheet.

You can't even keep it in your pocket!

HAVE A GO ...

Collect some data – a pocket money budget is easy to work out. Give yourself a fixed amount and decide how much to spend on different things. Add your data to a spreadsheet program and create a pie chart using the data. Now try to draw the pie chart. What differences do you notice?

QUICK TEST

1. When should you use a bar chart?

2. When should you use a pie chart?

3. When should you use a line graph?

ANSWERS 1. To make comparisons between two (or more) sets of data. **2.** When something is divided up into several sections. **3.** For investigations involving time.

PARTY TIME

It's almost your birthday and you have been promised a whole class party, because it will be the last birthday you have in your primary school. There are 28 people in your class

Your two best friends are going to help you plan everything, but you have been given a budget, £150 maximum, and you can't go over it. The party is to be held in your garden, so it won't cost anything to hire somewhere. But you need food and drink for everyone, plus invitations and party prizes. How are you going to keep within your budget?

WHAT SHOULD YOU BUY?

First, you need to make a list of everything you need and how much it costs. You're not sure what everyone likes, so you decide to carry out a sandwich survey to make sure you only have the most popular choices.

Design a questionnaire that asks your class mates which sandwiches and drinks they like. Your friends are going to help you transfer the information to a database.

Name	Emergency contact	Favourite sandwich	2nd Choice of sandwich	Favourite drink	2nd Choice of drink

If you have a class record for everyone in your class, then you could make a note of emergency contact phone numbers just in case of a problem at the party. Promise that you'll get rid of them as soon as the party is over, and you won't pass them onto anybody – you've got to respect other people's privacy. Many people won't give out home or mobile phone numbers, in case they are found abd used by an unknown party.

When all the data is in the database, use it to make some graphs showing favourite sandwiches and favourite drinks to help you plan what to buy.

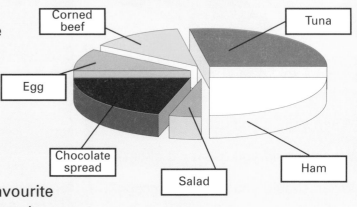

HANDLING INFORMATION INVESTIGATION

COSTS

What can you use to find out how much the food, the drink, the gifts and the invites will cost? A spreadsheet of course! That way, you can keep an eye on your budget total as you go along.

As you buy things, change the estimated figures into real figures. If you find the budget is creeping too near the total, perhaps you can change what's on your list to something cheaper.

Mel had a party last year. Here are her figures to help you.

She kept to her budget, but the costs may be different for your party. Check out the prices at the supermarket.

You may also decide to have different food. Mel had pizza, but you might choose to have hot dogs. How would that affect your figures?

Has Mel missed anything you would include?

Comic Sans MS — 12 — **B** *I*

D19 ▼ = =SUM(D3:[

	A	B per unit	C no of units	D costs
1	Party Budget			
2		per unit	no of units	costs
3	cola	1.25	12	15.00
4	orange	1.25	12	15.00
5	bread	0.60	4	2.40
6	tuna	0.75	5	3.75
7	eggs (doz)	1.20	2	2.40
8	ham	1.20	4	4.80
9	pizza	2.50	5	12.50
10	choc rolls	0.99	5	4.95
11	cakes	0.99	2	1.98
12	biscuits	1.50	3	4.50
13	invites	0.30	28	8.40
14	party gifts	2.00	28	56.00
15	prizes for games	0.50	10	5.00
16	birthday cake	2.00	4	8.00
17	butter	2.50	1	2.50
18				
19			Total no	147.18

TEST ROUND-UP

SECTION 1

Type these words into a spreadsheet using the cell references.

A3	bags	D1	for	F5	and	B2	met
F6	and	B7	each	C6	had	D3	each
B1	I	A2	I	D5	three	F3	were
E2	with	E3	bag	B5	collar	A6	each
C1	went	F7	whisker!	E6	holes	C7	hole
D2	man	D7	was	A7	in	B6	bell
A1	When	D4	each	D6	two	E7	a
E1	a	B3	and	B4	cats	C2	a
C5	with	A4	four	F1	walk	F2	five
E5	bells	C4	and	C3	in	E4	cat
A5	a	F4	had				

1. Who went for a walk?
2. How many bells were there?

_____

_____

SECTION 2

Fill in the missing words.

1. A record is made up of different _____.

2. A group of records is called a _____.

3. To find information on a database, you have to _____ and _____.

4. A _____ _____ helps you to sort and classify information.

5. A spreadsheet displays data in _____ and _____ .

70

SECTION 3

Name these tools or parts of a spreadsheet.

1. _____

2. _____

3. _____

4. _____

5. _____

6. _____

7. _____

SECTION 4

1. Name three types of graphs or charts.

_____

_____

_____

2. Which would you use to show how you spend your pocket money?

_____

3. Which would you use to record the temperature in a room during a school day?

_____

EXPLORING SIMULATIONS

SIMULATIONS

A <u>computer simulation</u> allows you to study or try things that would be difficult or impossible to do in real life. A simulation program *lets you make choices from the safety of a computer screen*, so you can, for example, swim with sharks, investigate how the human body works, experience walking with dinosaurs or build an adventure playground. Many of the games played from a <u>CD-ROM</u> simulate these types of activities.

In the real world, simulations are carried out in real jobs, too. Pilots train in a simulator, architects test their designs using models before building the real thing and scientists test products in safe laboratories for many years before making their discoveries available to others.

Where else do you think simulations might be useful?

top tip

When working with a simulation try to answer this question: Have you learnt something by using a model that you didn't know before?

REAL OR IMAGINARY?

Some simulations feel very real – a flight simulator, for example. Others, such as adventure games, are lots of fun and often very exciting, but definitely imaginary! The characters never get tired, they never stop and eat, and they often wear the same clothes whatever the weather!

LEARNING FROM A SIMULATION

Sam and Mel are using a simulation program to investigate the conditions needed to grow a plant. They have watched real plants growing and think they need water and sunlight, but are not sure how much. The simulation program lets them try out different growing conditions. It lets them change:

- where the plant is grown
- the time of year
- the amount of water the plant gets
- the type of food the plant gets.

They watch and record what happens to the plant in each different situation. From their results they can begin to explore patterns and relationships, and they can predict which conditions will help the plant grow best.

After their experiments Sam and Mel were asked these questions.

- 'Was the model you set up realistic?' They thought it was.
- 'Did the same things always happen – was there a pattern?' They thought there was. The plant they chose always grew better when it was warmer, when it had water, when it was sunny and when it was fed.
- 'Were the simulation experiments helpful?' They thought they were. The simulation helped to predict how much sunlight and water the plant needed and the best time of year to put it outside.
- 'How could it be improved?' They thought it would be interesting to do the experiment again with a different type of plant.

Dad's taking us on a flight simulator.

Do I need a passport?

QUICK TEST

1. What does a simulation program let you do?

2. When might a simulation program be used in real life?

ANSWERS 1. It lets you try things out that would be difficult or impossible to do in real life. 2. Pilots and astronauts use simulators.

HAVE A GO ...

Think about a simulation activity you would like to try. Ask yourself what is this activity going to let me do? Why is it safer to do this with a computer? What do I hope to learn?

ENTERING FORMULAE

Spreadsheets use *simple formulae* to help with *calculations*. Remember all formulae begin with =.

Here is a spreadsheet formula for 20 ÷ 4: **=A3/B3**.
Type the formula into **C3** and press **Enter** and you can see the answer 5.

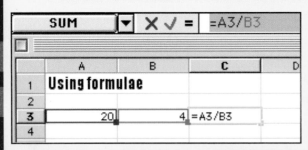

AREA AND PERIMETER

Let's look at some more formulae.

The formula for the area of a rectangle is **l x b**.
Let's put that into the spreadsheet shown below. The formula is **=C4*D4**.
Type the formula into **E4** and press **Enter** and you can see the answer 20.

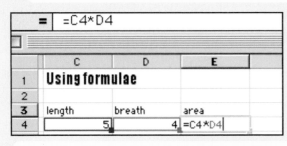

The formula for the perimeter of a rectangle is **2 x (l + b)**.
Let's put that into a spreadsheet. The formula is **=2*(C4+D4)**.

Another way to write this is **=2*SUM(C4:D4)**.
Type the formula into **F4** and press **Enter** and you can see the answer 18.

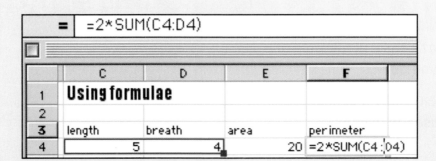

MODEL BEHAVIOUR

CHANGING VARIABLES

Rectangles vary in size. In spreadsheet language, we would say that the length and breadth are <u>variables</u> because they can change. Try changing the numbers in cells **C4** and **D4**. What happens when you press **Enter**?

The numbers in **E4** and **E5** change. The spreadsheet uses the formulae to *recalculate the perimeter and the area* with the new figures for the length and breadth. This happens every time you change the length and breadth.

COPYING FORMULAE

Spreadsheets let you copy formulae from *one cell to another*. Look at this carefully, then try it for yourself.

	A	B	C
1			
2			
3			
4	2	4	=A4*B4
5	4	8	
6	6	12	

Multiply Column A by Column B using a formula in Column C. The first one has been done for you, **=A4*B4**.

Using **Copy** 📋 and **Paste** 📋, copy the formula from **C4** to **C5**, **C6**, **C7** and **C8**. Watch what happens.

The whole table has been completed. Notice that the formula for each cell appears in the **Formula** bar while the result of the formula, the number, appears in the cell. The formula changes as it is copied to recognise that it is multiplying different cell references. In this example the formula for **C8** is **A8*B8**.

C8	▼	=	=A8*B8

	A	B	C
1			
2			
3			
4	2	4	8
5	4	8	32
6	6	12	72
7	8	16	128
8	10	20	200

QUICK TEST

1. What do formulae help with in a spreadsheet?

2. Spreadsheets allow you to copy formula from one cell to another; true or false?

3. What can help you to understand the information better on a spreadsheet?

ANSWERS 1. = 2. True. 3. A graph.

HAVE A GO ...

Try some calculations. Open a spreadsheet and entre ten figures in column A and column B. Then put a formulae into C1 and copy and past it into C2 to C10!

75

MODELLING INVESTIGATION

THE PROBLEM

A farmer wants to put a fence around a new rectangular paddock for his bull. The perimeter is 20m, but he's not sure how long and wide to make it. He wants a paddock with the maximum area possible inside the perimeter.

BUILDING A SPREADSHEET MODEL

The farmer knows that to calculate the area of the paddock, he needs to use the formula **l x b**.

He knows that to calculate the perimeter of the paddock, he needs to use the formula **2 x (l + b)**.

He set up a spreadsheet like this.

	A	B	C	D
1	Farmer's Paddock			
2				
3	Perimeter	20m		
4				
5				
6	length	breadth	perimeter	area
7				

I bet I'm smarter at area calculation than you are.

That's not true - I know the fridge area off by heart!

INVESTIGATE

Using the spreadsheet, add the variables for the length and the breadth. The farmer only wants to use whole metres, not parts of a metre, in his calculations. He has to remember that the perimeter is 2 x (l + b) and that this must always add up to 20m.

	A	B	C	D
1	Farmer's Paddock			
2				
3	Perimeter	20m		
4				
5				
6	length	breadth	perimeter	area
7	9	1	20	
8	8	2	20	
9				

- Add all the numbers possible in columns A and B.
- Type in a formula for the perimeter in column C (If you have the right numbers in columns A and B, the answer will always be 20).
- Type in a formula to work out the area in column D.

RESULT

What is the length and breadth of the rectangle that gives you the biggest area?

What have you found out about this rectangle?

To see your result on a graph, use the chart icon. Your chart should look like this:

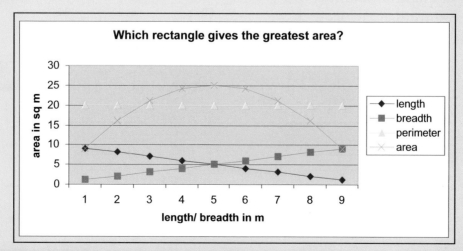

TEST ROUND-UP

SECTION 1

	A	B	C
1			
2	23	2	46
3	46	4	
4	33	6	198
5	22	8	176
6	89	2	178
7	12	4	48
8	35	3	

1. Look at this example. Work out which formula was used to get the answer in C2. _____

2. Using the same formula can you predict the answer for C3. _____

3. Predict the answer for C8. _____

4. If the formula in C5 was changed to =A7/B7, what would the number change to in C7? _____

5. If the formula in C5 was changed to SUM(A5:B5) what would the number change to in C5? _____

SECTION 2

	A	B	C	D
1				
2				
3	length	breadth	area	perimeter
4	6		24	20
5		10	190	58
6	15	6	90	42
7	11	7	77	
8	45	20		130
9				

Look at this example. Which formula was used to calculate the answer?

1. in C7 _____

2. in D5 _____

3. in C4 _____

4. in D8 _____

5. in D6 _____

What number is missing

6. in B4 _____

7. in D7 _____

8. in C8 _____

9. in A5 _____

YOU'RE IN CONTROL

You have :
- 3 light bulbs red, orange and green
- a buzzer
- a control box with four outputs numbered 1, 2, 3, and 4.

Give each bulb and the buzzer a number to match each of the sockets:

- 1 = red
- 2 = amber
- 3 = green
- 4 = buzzer.

Write procedures in control language for each part of the sequence. Here's the first part to help you. Use a new line for each new action, for example:

- Turn off 1 Turn on 2
- Wait 3
- Turn off 2 Turn on 3
- Turn on 4.

Use wait so that your light stays on for a few seconds, or it will just flash on and off. Remember in a real situation the traffic needs time to stop.

TRYING IT OUT

If possible, try out the procedures using a control box and a computer, or a simulation program.

Did you need to make any changes to your procedures?

I wonder if there's a procedure for dealing with pesky brothers?

It would take more than a control box to make me behave!

TEST ROUNDUP

SECTION 1

What shape would the screen turtle draw with these procedures?

1. fd 150, rt 90, fd 150, rt 90,
   fd 150, rt 90, fd 150, rt 90

   _____

2. rt 90, fd 50, lt 90, fd 50, lt 90,
   fd 50, rt 90, fd 50, rt 90, fd 50

   _____

3. fd 200, rt 120, fd 200, rt 120,
   fd 200, rt 120

   _____

4. repeat 4, [fd 100, lt 90]

   _____

5. repeat 3 [fd 150, rt 120]

   _____

SECTION 2

Look at this course. It is 6 steps from A to B and 10 steps from B to C.

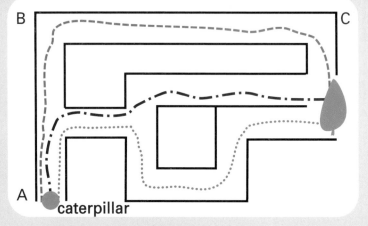

caterpillar

1. Write instructions for the caterpillar to get to the leaf on the red path.

   _____

   _____

2. Write instructions for the caterpillar to get to the leaf on the green path.

   _____

   _____

SECTION 3

True or false?

- It is possible to use simulation software instead of a Control Box to practise using inputs and outputs. _____

- Sensors are attached to the output sockets of a Control Box. _____

- Light sensors monitor temperature. _____

- Screen turtle steps are much smaller than floor turtle steps. _____

- Rt 90 is a right-angled turn. _____

SECTION 4

Fill in the gaps.

Command	Command
	Moves turtle back to its starting position
	turns right 90 – clockwise
lt 120	
fd 10	
	Moves back 20 steps
	Pen on screen ready to draw

TEST ROUND-UP ANSWERS

Introduction to ICT

Section 1
1. ICT stands for Information and Communication Technology.
2. All the bits and pieces of equipment are called hardware.
3. By holding the Shift Key, you can type capital letters and the symbols on the number keys.
4. DTP stand for Desk Top Publishing.
5. A CPU is a Central Processing Unit – this is the 'brains' inside a computer.

Section 2
What has changed in the 2nd sentence?
1. Colour for red and green. Capitals for stop and go.
2. The Font.
3. The text size.

Section 3
Which of these would you use a computer for?
1. no
2. maybe
3. yes
4. no
5. yes

Section 4
What are these used for?
1. A Spellchecker checks the spellings in a document.
2. A Thesaurus suggests new words with the same meaning as the original word.
3. Cut and paste lets you move letters, words, chunks of text or images from one place to another.
4. Search and Replace lets you find and change a word or words throughout a document.
5. Clip Art is a gallery of pictures, images and symbols. Pictures are selected from the gallery to add to a document.
6. Alignment places letters, words, chunks of text or images to the right, left or centre in a document.
7. Bullets are symbols like large dots that mark the start of an item in a list.
8. Columns arrange text in a newspaper style.
9. Text boxes are boxes inserted into a document that can contain text or images.
10. Scanners are used to scan images and photos into a computer.

Graphics

Section 1
1. Logos, illustrations, banners, or buttons.
2. Click on the line tool and hold the SHIFT key while dragging the mouse.
3. This is a shortcut to the drawing tools menu.
4. This is used to cut (take out) a piece of text or an image that has been highlighted.
5. By changing the shape of the brush using the options menu.

Section 2
1. Rubber/ Eraser.
2. Pencil tool.
3. Line tool.
4. Zoom/ magnifier to see an enlarged image.
5. Brush tool.
6. Text tool.

Section 3
How do you resize an image?
1. Add an image to a page using a Clip Art Gallery, a digital camera or a scanner.
2. Make sure the cursor is over the picture and click the right mouse button.
3. Choose Format Picture from the pop up menu.
4. Now select layout and choose a layout option – tight or square works well for most images – and click OK.
5. To make the picture bigger or smaller drag a corner 'handle'.

Section 4
1. To make a Repeat Pattern using a computer, Copy an image and Paste it several times horizontally, vertically or diagonally.
2. To make a Symmetrical Pattern using the computer, Copy an image, Paste it and Flip it, horizontally or vertically.
3. A Graphics Program uses layers. The layers are transparent. You can add, move and change images easily on each layer used, but you can always see a 'background' layer underneath that doesn't

change. Layers are useful when drawing plans or designing images.

Multimedia

Section 1
Tick the correct answer:
1a. Home Page link.
2b. A combination of sound, text, animation and video.
3b. Compact Disk, Read Only Memory.
4c. A hand.
5a. A colour wheel.

Section 2

N	O	T	T	U	B	I	O
A	M	X	S	L	I	D	E
T	E	G	M	I	T	I	G
T	S	O	U	N	D	E	A
A	M	E	S	U	D	M	P
N	I	D	I	A	I	L	B
M	P	I	C	T	U	R	E
E	I	V	O	M	A	N	W

Section 3
1. Home Button – takes you back to home page.
2. Link to video clip.
3. Link to sound clip.
4. Leave the program.
5. Back Button – takes you back to previous page you looked at.

Section 4
True or False?
1. True
2. False
3. False
4. True
5. True
6. True

Internet & Email

Section 1
Missing words
1. Computers
2. Multimedia
3. Favourites
4. World Wide Web
5. Mailbox

Section 2
1. Special pieces of software that let you see sound, video or some text files.
2. Chat rooms are 'areas' of the Internet where you can 'chat' to other people by typing comments via your keyboard.
3. Modems allow computers to 'talk' to each other. Most computers have modems inside them.
4. A Universal Resource Locator or a web address.
5. Something that attaches itself to emails and downloads. It can damage files on a computer.

Section 3
The answer is Internet.

Section 4
1. 30 Merchant Road, Level 3, Riverside Point.
2. A lunar eclipse happens when the Moon passes through the Earth's shadow.
3. 1819 – 1901. She became queen in 1837 and was queen for almost 64 years.
4. Straight lines, geometric shapes and the images of animals and birds carved on the ground that can only be seen from a plane.

Databases & Spreadsheets

Section 1
Spreadsheet story

When	I	went	for	a	walk
I	met	a	man	with	five
bags	and	in	each	bag	were
four	cats	and	each	cat	had
a	collar	with	three	bells	and
each	bell	had	two	holes	and
in	each	hole	was	a	whisker!

1. I went for a walk.
2. I found 60 bells.

Section 2
Missing words:
1. fields
2. file
3. search and sort
4. branching database
5. columns and rows

Section 3
Name the tools:
1. active cell
2. cell
3. autosum
4. chart wizard
5. formula bar
6. print
7. save

Section 4

Types of graph:

1. Block, Bar, Pie, Line or Scatter.

2. A Pie Chart.

3. A line graph.

Modelling

Section 1

1. =A2*B2

2. 184

3. 105

4. 3

5. 30

Section 2

Which formula was used to calculate the answer?

1. =A7*B7

2. =2*SUM(A5:B5)

3. =A4*B4

4. =2*SUM(A8:B8)

5. =2*SUM(A6:B6)

What number is missing?

6. 4

7. 36

8. 900

9. 19

Section 3

True or false?

1. true

2. false – it only appears in the formula bar when you press enter.

3. false

4. true

5. true

Section 4

Word search:

N	S	E	C	I	O	H	C
A	M	X	S	H	E	E	T
T	E	G	M	I	T	D	G
T	A	L	U	M	R	O	F
A	M	L	E	D	O	M	P
E	L	B	A	I	R	A	V
P	R	E	D	I	C	T	E
E	T	A	L	U	M	I	S

Control and Monitoring

Section 1

Which shape?

1. a square

2. letter s with vertical and horizontal lines

3. a triangle

4. a square

5. a triangle

Section 2

1. Forward 6
Right 90
Forward 10
Right 90
Forward 3

2. Forward 3
Right 90
Forward 2
Right 90
Forward 3
Left 90
Forward 4
Left 90
Forward 3
Right 90
Forward 4

Section 3

True or false?

• true

• false – they are input devices

• false - they monitor light

• true

• true

Section 4

The finished chart is:

Command	Action
home	Moves turtle back to its starting position
rt 90	Turns right 90° clockwise
lt 120	Turns left 120° anticlockwise
fd 10	Moves forward 10 steps
bk20	Moves back 20 steps
pd	Pen on screen ready to draw

GLOSSARY

<u>CD-ROM</u> (Compact Disk-Read Only Memory) Looks like a CD but it contains words and graphics as well as sound. CD-ROMs store large amounts of information.

<u>Chat Rooms</u> Chat rooms are meeting places on the Internet where you can send and receive messages, and read other people's messages. You should always be careful not to divulge any personal information about yourself and to use a nickname.

<u>Communication</u> In ICT, Communication refers to hardware that you use to communicate with others, such as a fax machine, mobile phone and email.

<u>Computer simulation</u> A simulation acts out real life or fantastic scenarios on a computer screen. A pilot uses computer simulations to learn how to fly a plane without any danger to himself or others.

<u>Control Box</u> A device with output and input sockets that connects to a computer. Instructions can be sent from the computer to the box to control lights, buzzers and motors plugged into the output sockets; instructions can be received by the computer through the box from sensors plugged into the input sockets.

<u>DTP</u> A computer application that helps you to change page layouts with graphics, images and words, in different sizes and styles.

<u>Edit</u> Editing your work means to correct spelling and punctuation so it reads properly and moving text around so it flows and is easy to understand.

<u>Hard disk</u> Found inside a computer. Used for storing large amounts of information.

<u>Hardware</u> All the mechanical and electronic bits and pieces that make up a computer system. For example, a keyboard and printer.

<u>Hyperlinks</u> Hyperlinks link web pages together. It is text or an image in a web page with particular formatting. When you clink on it, you are taken to a different part of that web page or another web page.

<u>Internet</u> A worldwide network of computers that provides a huge source of information. The computers are linked through modems and phone lines.

<u>Key words</u> Important words in a web page that describe its content. They make searching for a document much easier.

<u>Logo</u> A programming language used for school children to grasp programming skills.

<u>Mailbox</u> Software that allows you to send and receive email from a central

point, and find and sort them quickly and easily.

Microchips A microchip is a tiny CPU used in household equipment, the 'brains' of the equipment.

Microsoft PowerPoint Presentation software that allows you to incorporate multimedia such as text, sounds, pictures and video clips.

Modem A piece of hardware inside a computer used to send and receive information via a telephone line.

Multimedia A combination of words, sound, pictures and images – still and moving – controlled by a computer.

Presentation and authoring software Software used to create slide shows incorporating graphics and images and to write in certain formats. It is used in classrooms and business meetings.

Procedure A sequence of instructions or commands stored by a CPU that makes equipment work.

Sensors A device used to measure changes to light, temperature or sound. Sensors can be connected to control boxes or data-logging devices.

Spellcheck A tool to check spelling and suggest alternatives if the spelling is incorrect.

Symmetrical Having one line or more of symmetry means an object is identical on both sides of the line.

Thesaurus Useful tool that suggests alternatives to common words, so your writing is interesting and powerful.

Variables Data that can change. We would say that the information in a spreadsheet is variable if it is constantly updated.

Word-processing A computer program used for writing, editing, saving and printing words.

World Wide Web A large, international library with millions of pages of information, accessed via the internet.